Jean Dancy's

LOVE GUIDE

FOR

TEENS

By Jean Dancy

Relationship Counselor

Copyright ©2022 by Jean Dancy

All rights reserved.
No portion of this book may be reproduced, stored in a retrieval system, or transmitted in any form or by any means—electronic, mechanical, photo copy, recording, scanning, or other—except for brief quotations in critical reviews or articles, without the prior written permission of the creator, Jean Dancy, or the Editor, Ava Monroe.
For Permissions please contact:
Inhousepublishinginfo@gmail.com

Published by InHouse Publishing
Printed in the United States of America.
Cover concept and design: Ava Monroe
Editor: Ava Monroe
ISBN: 978-1-7377288-18

To Reach Jean Dancy:
InHouse Publishing
Inhousepublishinginfo@gmail.com
Instagram: @JeanDancy

To my precious daughter,
Ava...

My baby
My blessing
My best friend

You Will Discover:

*How to tell if it is "temporary" love or the love that will last forever.

*Why real love never hurts.

*The 10 Commandments that people who love you will never break.

*How to identify controlling people.

*How to identify potential abusers.

*Statements that abusers use.

CONTENTS

Introduction ... 1

Chapter 1: Teen Love—Unconditional Love ... 9

Chapter 2: Love ... 19

Chapter 3: "Blove" ... 27

Chapter 4: Does Love Ever Hurt? ... 37

Chapter 5: The Words, "I Love You" ... 45

Chapter 6: You Cannot Make Anyone Like You ... 53

Chapter 7: We Teach People How to Treat Us ... 61

Chapter 8: Things Boys Say to Get Sex from Girls ... 69

Chapter 9: Potential Signs of an Abusive Boyfriend   77

Chapter 10: Things that Controlling
Abusive Boyfriends May Say   85

Chapter 11: Physical Abuse   93

Chapter 12: Ten Commandments of Teen Love   101

Teen Check List   109

You Are Precious   115

A Conversation with Jean Dancy   119

About the Author   123

Introduction

When this book first came out, I was still teaching English at Cleveland High School in California. This book was my baby, my gift... to all of the teenage girls who were crowding my room and following me across the campus... pleading with me for answers, "Ms. Dancy, Ms. Dancy! What is *real* love?"

This book answers that question and so much more...as it uncovers the lies, tricks, and traps often set for girls.

I got an opportunity to see how my book affected them after they read it. I heard the following things from students:

Your book really helped me! Within two weeks my boyfriend told me that I couldn't wear my hair down, that I couldn't wear lip gloss, or spend time with my friends. Your book taught me that his behavior is controlling behavior.

Before I read your book, I bought my boyfriend presents and I gave him money because I thought those things would make him like me better. They didn't.

I was trying to control my girlfriend; but I couldn't see it until I read your book.

Nothing has changed. Why? Because there will *ALWAYS* be boys—who use the original—tried and true lies (that I share in this book)—to control unsuspecting girls and get money, sex, and other things from them.

And there will *ALWAYS* be girls who are hearing the lies for the first time. Those who believe the lies may suffer consequences that will last a lifetime.

I have watched the parade of unhappy girls—turned women on TV shows—regurgitating all of the "lines" that were used to entrap them.

They were once innocent, unsuspecting girls who had no idea that they were being used. They were once in an ocean of girls; and the boys used whatever line the girls needed to hear in order to catch the girls.

Some were left with babies, and some were left with maybes. *Maybe the next boy will love me...*

It is my desire now...as it was then, to educate girls about the tricks and traps that some boys set for them. It is also my goal to educate boys about the traps that they set for girls that may leave the boys locked up themselves.

This book was originally written because of an incident that happened between Chris Brown and Rihanna.

They were in the news every day and my students were confused and disillusioned about love.

The thought that Chris could actually abuse Rihanna was more than they could comprehend. I answered questions and gave advice about "teen love" every day. Students from other classes and other schools were stopping by my room asking for advice.

My wonderful students at Cleveland High said, "Ms. Dancy, you should write something for us to follow...something short and very easy to understand."

That is how this book was born.

I have counseled married couples, troubled teens, and people with relationship problems for years. Relationships and all of their intricacies fascinate me.

I love teenagers and I consider it an honor and a privilege to be in their presence. I am in awe of how beautiful they are and I wish I could show the world what I see behind those tattoos, sagging clothes, and pierced bodies.

Although this book was written primarily to help teenage girls identify some of the lies, tricks, and traps of abusers; it can be a valuable tool for young men to see where they are on the potentially abusive scale.

Some people toss the thought of teen love out of their minds like a used coffee cup but it's real... so real that there are young people who consider suicide when it ends. I know.

I have talked with them. I have cried with them.

My first love was the center of my teen universe and I have diaries to prove how profoundly that relationship affected me. Our love story was much like a fairy-tale, thanks to my mother's guidance and the fact that our feelings for each other were mutual. All stories don't have happy endings though.

This book can be a treasure for precious girls who are stumbling through those wonderful butterfly feelings of love without a flashlight or a plan.

Love Guide for Teens provides clear, simple information, a roadmap, and a flashlight that can help guide teenagers through their journey---**unharmed**.

Teens need to know that certain things from life's menu can affect them for the rest of their lives. They need to know that some desserts were not made for them...not because the cook is mean but because the cook loves them...and knows what they can digest.

This book does **not** promote or endorse inappropraiate behavior for teenagers.

Love can always wait... But lust is always in a hurry.

Chapter 1

Teen Love — Unconditional Love

Those breathtaking butterfly feelings and honey coated hugs that teenagers share...as wonderful as they feel...are usually temporary. I don't say that in an effort to diminish them but in an effort to warn someone who believes those feelings will last forever. Sometimes they last for years (as mine did) and sometimes they only last until a cuter girl appears or a better-looking boy passes by.

One of my students had been with her boyfriend for over a year. She told me on many occasions how very much they loved each other. I walked by them gazing into each other's eyes every day. Later in the year, she cried in disbelief as she said, "Ms. Dancy, my boyfriend met a new girl last week and now he says he loves her."

She was shocked because she thought they would graduate together in a couple of years, go to college together, and marry in front of all of their family and friends.

She had even named their first son (imaginary of course!) after him! It is not unusual for some girls to take it that far. My boyfriend's name was written on everything I owned, and I couldn't eat if we were unhappy with each other.

If young people are taught (as I was) that teen love and unconditional love are not the same, they can be prepared for the possible twists and turns in the journey. Aaaaah...I can hear a fifteen-year-old girl saying, "I don't care what anybody says, my boyfriend and I will be together forever. He will never cheat on me and he loves me unconditionally!"

I hope that what they have will graduate into unconditional love. However, teenagers aren't usually equipped to hold unconditional love any more than a cup is equipped to hold an ocean.

Teen love is sometimes based on looks, a certain body type, or popularity...dating the football player, etc. It is often fueled by raw emotion...I hate you on Monday but I love you on Tuesday. It can be a roller coaster ride based solely on the feelings of the moment.

Because teen love doesn't have adequate light, teenagers who can't see around the corner, want to have a baby together. There's no rational thought regarding income, the responsibility of another human being for at least 18 years, how it will affect their lives, or their parents' lives.

Americans use the word "love" so loosely: *"I love my cake, I love my car, I love my child, I love my parents, I love my candy."* They use the word as if all types of love fall into the same category. In the Greek language there are different words to express different kinds of love.

Eros needs certain circumstances and situations to be right or the relationship could end. It is sexual, romantic, and passionate in nature.

Philia expresses friendship or brotherly love.

Storge is the kind of love that parents have for their children.

Agape is referred to as the God kind of love because it is spiritual, self-giving, unconditional, the highest and purest form of love, voluntary, and never ending. It is the forever kind of love.

In Greek terms, teen love usually falls neatly under the "Eros" category. However, I have another name for it (more about that later).

What are some of the differences between teen love and unconditional love?

Was there a time when you believed that all love was the same?

NOTES

Love is the most expensive gift that you will ever give.

Chapter 2

Love...

Love is the best thing that the world has to offer. There is nothing bigger...and there is nothing better! Real love is always unconditional and it has certain characteristics that will help you distinguish it from all other things.

1. Love is patient.

2. Love is kind.

3. Love is not jealous, boastful, or rude.

4. Love does not demand its own way.

5. Love is not irritable, and it keeps no record of when it has been wronged.

6. Love is never glad about injustice but rejoices whenever the truth wins out.

7. Love never gives up.

8. Love never loses faith.

9. Love is always hopeful.

10. Love endures through every circumstance.

11. Love will last **forever!**

12. **Love never fails!**

What are some of the characteristics of love?

Do you believe that most teenagers are ready for unconditional love?

NOTES

*When you know what love is...
you will know what it is not.*

Chapter 3

"Blove"

Unconditional love never fails, however there is something that always fails. I call it "blove" because people who are in it sincerely believe they are in love. They are not. Blove is a temporary feeling that is often mistaken for love and it has characteristics that clearly distinguish it as well.

1. Blove is not patient.

2. Blove is not kind.

3. Blove is always jealous.

4. Blove keeps a record of everything that goes wrong.

5. Blove always demands its own way.

6. Blove has lies.

7. Blove has deception.

8. Blove can cross all boundaries. A person who bloves you can date your best friend, your sister, your brother, or your spouse.

9. Blove is fueled by lust.

10. Blove gives up when things are no longer easy.

11. Blove is very unforgiving.

12. Blove is always temporary.

People who are in blove have no problem hurting you. Blove's foundation is selfishness. Those who love you can always put your best interest first. Those who blove you are incapable of putting your best interest first. It's always about what they want for themselves.

People in blove are often unhappy internally. In an effort to divert attention from their imperfections, they constantly point the finger at others—pointing out what's wrong with them. Nothing is ever quite good enough for some blovers.

Other blovers are nice, polite people, who just thought they were in love. The bottom line with both groups of people is the same—time. Blove always has an expiration date on it.

Blovers are not capable of making a lifetime commitment and keeping it. Therefore the feeling that once held the couple together will definitely end.

It may last for weeks, months, or even years, but the feeling will evaporate. Some who started out bloving each other end up hating each other.

Do you believe that most teenagers are in love or in "blove?"

What are the things that stand out most in your mind about "blove?"

NOTES

When you love yourself... you will not harm yourself.

Chapter 4

Does Love Ever Hurt?

No...not ever!!!!

Love seems to hurt when people don't understand how it works. A person says he loves you, he hurts you, and "love" gets the blame. In reality, *he* hurt you...love did not. If you are moaning and groaning over a boy who dumped you, remember, love didn't dump you—he did. Love didn't create your moan or your groan. The action of your boyfriend dumping you caused that feeling.

If your boyfriend says, " I love you and you're the only girl for me," then he calls you stupid, says nobody will ever want you, and slaps you, remember...love is kind. Those cruel words don't come from a kind place.

They come from a negative selfish place. If those words hurt, don't forget that love didn't speak those words and love did not slap you. Could your boyfriend be in blove? Check its characteristics.

Do you believe that love hurts?

List a few situations in which love appears to hurt?

_____

_____

_____

_____

_____

_____

_____

_____

_____

_____

NOTES

Real love is known by the way it acts…not just by the way it talks.

Chapter 5

The Words, "I Love You"

The words, "I love you" have absolutely no meaning unless they are also accompanied by loving kind actions. Look at what he does—not what he says!

Words:	**Actions:**
I love you.	He hits you.
I love you.	He kicks you.
I love you.	He calls you negative names.
I love you.	He never calls or visits unless he wants something.

It is very simple, just look at the **actions**!!!

Do you know people who say, "I love you," but their behavior says something else?

_____

_____

_____

_____

_____

_____

_____

_____

_____

_____

_____

If a person is unkind to you most of the time, what kind of message does that send?

NOTES

There is only one wonderful "You" in the whole world!

Chapter 6

You Cannot Make Anyone Like You

You cannot make a boy like you—no matter what you do! Either he likes you or he doesn't. You are either his type or—you are not!

Think of it this way, if you hated spinach you probably would not eat it. However, if someone asked you to eat a bowl of spinach and that person also offered to give exactly what you wanted in exchange, it could become something you might consider doing. A boy may not like you any more than he likes spinach but the payoff of sex with you could cause him to spend time with you.

You still wouldn't be his type and he wouldn't suddenly like you any better. If he keeps coming back for more, it's only because he likes the sex—not YOU! Don't believe me?

Put it to the test. Stop the sex and he will never be with you again if he really doesn't like you.

Don't be fooled. If a boy likes you and you are his exact type, you don't have to do anything. It's already done—he likes you.

It's like cheesecake and me. It doesn't have to sing or dance for me. I just like it.

My dear, if he doesn't like you, move on. Don't attempt the impossible. You are someone's *exact* type.

10 Worst things a Girl can do (trying to get a boy to like her):

1. Have sex (intercourse).

2. Participate in any kind of sex...with any part of her body.

3. Text sex messages (Sexting), e-mail them, or convey them by any means.

4. Send nude or semi-nude pictures through the phone, or through the Internet, or by any means whatsoever.

5. Give money.

6. Buy clothes.

7. Smoke marijuana or vape any substance.

8. Drink alcohol.

9. Use pills or any other kind of drug.

10. Pretend to be someone other than who you really are.

Can you make anyone love you?

If you had an unlimited amount of money to give someone, do you think the person would start to like you?

_____

_____

_____

_____

_____

_____

_____

_____

_____

_____

_____

NOTES

Love yourself.
Cherish yourself.
You are worth it.

Chapter 7

We Teach People How to Treat Us

What you accept—and do nothing about—is what you have taught. If a boy hits you and you accept it—you have taught him that it's okay to hit you. If he calls you negative names—and you accept it—you have taught him to continue. If he only calls or comes around when he wants something—and you accept it—you have taught him to treat you that way.

Remember: What you accept—and do nothing about—is what you have taught.

> What you accept
> + Do nothing about
> ―――――――――――
> = What you have taught

Is there a connection between how people treat you—and the way you treat yourself?

If you love yourself and treat yourself with respect, is it likely to have an influence on the way people treat you?

NOTES

When you understand your value... you will not spend your life foolishly.

Chapter 8

Things Boys Say to Get Sex from Girls

1. If you love me—prove it.

2. You can't get pregnant the first time.

3. You're the only girl I love.

4. I plan to marry you someday.

5. If you don't have sex with me, I'll have to leave you and go with a girl who will.

6. Everybody's doing it.

7. If you love me—like I love you—you will have sex with me.

8. I don't even want to use protection with you because I love you and I would marry you if you became pregnant.

9. If you have sex with me, I won't have any need to have sex with anyone else.

10. I only want to have sex with you because I love you.

11. I'm a virgin too (a lie of course). Let's have our first sexual experience together.

12. I was only with that girl for sex. I don't like her. You're the only one I really love. If you have sex with me, I will never be with her again.

List five of the word "tricks" that some young men use to get sex.

Which word "trick" do you think works best?
Why do you believe that it works best?

NOTES

You can never put another person down... without becoming lower yourself.

Chapter 9

Potential Signs of an Abusive Boyfriend

Many potentially abusive boyfriends are also controlling. It usually starts with verbal abuse. He may call you the famous "b" word that rhymes so well with witch.

Put downs may follow:

1. You're too fat.

2. You're too skinny.

3. I don't like your clothes.

4. I don't like your hair.

5. You're stupid!

6. You're dumb.

Alienation often follows. He tries to separate you from your friends and family.

List some examples of verbal abuse.

Can verbal abuse also have a painful, lasting effect on people?

NOTES

Negative people are contagious! Stay away from them.

Chapter 10

Things that Controlling Abusive Boyfriends May Say:

1. You better not look at him.

2. You can't go to the party.

3. You can't be with those friends.

4. You can't wear that again.

5. You better do what I tell you to do.

6. You can't wear your hair like that.

7. Be home when I call you.

8. Let me see your phone—who did you call? Who did you text? What were you talking about?

9. You don't need anybody but me.

10. I own you—you belong to me.

11. Nobody else wants you.

12. I don't want you to wear make-up. Who are you trying to look good for?

Is anyone trying to control you?

List some of the things that a controlling person may say?

_____

_____

_____

_____

_____

_____

_____

_____

_____

_____

_____

NOTES

The seeds that you plant as a teenager—are the same ones that will be used to make a harvest when you are grown.

Chapter 11

Physical Abuse

Physical abuse is often gradual and it usually gets worse each time it happens. Those abusers may say the following:

1. You made me hit you.

2. It's your fault.

3. If you would just do as I tell you, I wouldn't hit you.

4. I will never do it again.

5. You made me lose my temper.

6. Get out of my face with that black eye.

7. I guess you're satisfied now.

8. You got what you asked for.

9. Don't make me hit you again.

10. When you change, I won't hit you anymore.

11. You just don't do things the right way.

12. You're the problem.

Abusers rarely take responsibility for their actions. They act as if their hands belong to you. In their minds, *you* made everything happen!

Has anyone ever slapped, pushed, or physically abused you in any way?

What kind of boyfriend would abuse his girlfriend?

NOTES

When you love yourself enough, you will not allow others to lead you astray.

Chapter 12

Ten Commandments of Teen Love

1. Thou shall not offer sex to me.

2. Thou shall not offer drugs to me.

3. Thou shall not offer alcohol to me.

4. Thou shall not hit me or physically abuse me in any way.

5. Thou shall not call me out of my name or verbally abuse me.

6. Thou shall not ask me to disobey my parents or guardians.

7. Thou shall not ask me to skip school.

8. Thou shall not harm my life.

9. Thou shall not harm my future.

10. Thou shall not ask me to be dishonest.

Do you know people who try to get others to break the Ten Commandments of Teen Love?

List the three Ten Commandments of Teen Love that you believe are broken most often?

_____

_____

_____

_____

_____

_____

_____

_____

_____

_____

NOTES

*You are too wonderful
to be used or abused!*

Teen Check List

1. Is he trying to get me to do things that make me feel uncomfortable? Is he trying to get me to do things that I feel are wrong?

2. Is he trying to get me involved in drugs?

3. Is he trying to get me involved in sex?

4. Is he trying to turn me against my parents or guardians?

5. Is he trying to keep me from spending time with my friends?

6. Is he trying to control me?

7. Is he trying to change my personality?

8. Does he call me out of my name?

9. Does he make negative jokes about me?

10. Does he make statements that are intended to put me down?

11. Have I begun to feel worse about myself when I'm around him?

12. Is he trying to get me to break *any* of the Ten commandments of Teen Love?

Just sharing: I will never forget a statement that my "first love," (Earl) made. It's in one of my diaries and it still amazes me. He said, "Jean, if I ask you to do something that your mother thinks you shouldn't do...don't do it. Go with what she says. Always take her word over everybody else's word—even mine. Nobody...will ever love you...more than your mother loves you."

You are a part of a universal puzzle that cannot be replaced or erased.

You Are Precious

You are an original...priceless and precious... the only one that the world has, a treasure whose gifts and talents may not have blossomed yet.

You are a part of the garden called "humanity" and if you are watered properly—someday you will bless the world with your fragrance.

Do you think of yourself as precious?

There is no excuse for teen abuse!

A Conversation with Jean Dancy

Question: Why did you write this book?

Answer: I was getting so many questions from teenagers after the Chris Brown, Rihanna incident. Teenagers that I knew were being abused by their boyfriends! One of my students, a lovely young lady, showed me pictures of her face after a beating from her boyfriend. Her face looked worse than Rihanna's. A court date was pending. Some of the things that I heard totally shocked me.

Question: What were some of the most shocking things that you heard?

Answer: Some girls didn't consider being slapped, physical abuse. "He just slapped me," they said. "It wasn't physical abuse."

Others didn't know that being called the "b" word is verbal abuse. Another very shocking thing to me was that so many girls thought they could do things to make boys like them.

They thought giving sex, sending nude pictures, giving gifts, and giving money would cause boys to like them better.

I found out that most parents are not addressing this subject and girls, in particular, are left totally uninformed and harmed.

Question: How did you come up with the Ten Commandments of Teen Love?

Answer: I thought if teens had something concrete, something they could refer to or possibly memorize, it would really help them.

Question: What do you hope to accomplish with this book?

Answer: I would like to put a spotlight on teen abuse and I would also like to provide information that will help alleviate the problem.

Question: What do you see as the biggest reason for teen abuse?

Answer: I think the biggest reason for teen abuse is a lack of education on the subject. It isn't being talked about enough; and teenagers are walking around without any armor.

Question: What are the future consequences if this subject isn't taken more seriously?

Answer: An abused teenager is the perfect candidate to become an abused adult. This is a very serious subject and it simply must be addressed properly.

About The Author

Muhammad Ali fascinated a little girl with his fancy footwork in the ring and caused her to fall in love with the sport of boxing. Her biggest dream was to meet Ali. Though destiny had something even better in mind. That little girl was Jean Dancy.

The Alabama A&M University graduate studied English and Psychology. She is grateful to have worked as an Actress, Model, Make-up Artist, Jazz Singer, English Teacher, Sportswriter, Motivational Speaker, Life Skills Teacher, Real Estate Broker, and Certified Mediator.

However, her most outstanding accomplishment happened when she made boxing history by becoming the only woman to become both a Boxing Manager and a Boxing Promoter. Additionally, Jean is the first female to manage and later promote an athlete who was also her husband. Under Dancy's management, Marty Monroe soared to a #4 world ranking in the Heavyweight boxing division.

Throughout her career, Dancy has received recognition for her achievements.

Some of those achievements include being named "Woman of the Year" in sports for her accomplishments in the boxing business; and being honored for becoming a member of the multi-million dollar circle of salespeople as a Real Estate Broker.

What about Muhammad Ali?—and destiny? Jean didn't just meet Ali, she became the only female boxing manager in his Deer Lake Training Camp!

As a Sportswriter and boxing enthusiast, Dancy has interacted with some of the most elite boxers, trainers, and promoters in the history of the sport. That list includes Muhammad Ali, Joe Frazier, George Foreman, Roberto Duran, Don King, Evander Holyfield, Thomas "Hit Man" Hearns, the Mayweathers, and many more.

Jean Dancy is the mother of a lovely daughter named Ava. She particularly enjoys helping people in relationships, motivational speaking, singing, and painting.

Please also enjoy!…

Muhammad Ali and Me

by Jean Dancy

"Muhammad Ali and Me"
By Jean Dancy

THERE IS NO bigger name or icon on planet Earth than Muhammad Ali (among mere human beings); and despite the odds, God allowed my footsteps to meet at the same place…and at the same time…with his footsteps.

My biggest dream—in life—was to meet Ali, but God had something far greater in mind.

This is the story of a little girl who wanted to meet Muhammad Ali…the lengths she took on that journey…and what happened when her dream finally came true.

Available on Amazon, Barnes and Noble, and online everywhere books are sold.

10 TIPS ON
How to Live a Stress-FREE *Life!*

By Jean Dancy

"10 Tips on How to Live a Stress-Free Life!"

By Jean Dancy

People can frantically flap their arms trying desperately to swim upstream—or they can get into a canoe of peace and glide smoothly over the waves of life.

We do not live in a perfect world; but we can find ways to handle this imperfect world more effectively.

Though it may not seem like it, happiness really is a choice. However, living a peaceful, stress-free life isn't an arbitrary destination where one ends up without effort. No. It takes practice and I am here to make it easy for you.

This is a simple book…filled with quick nutritious snacks that will help you live a happier, healthier life!

Choose to be happy. Choose to be peaceful. Choose to be stress-free!

MY BLACK KING

By Jean Dancy

"My Black King"
By Jean Dancy

My Black King is a poignant and soul-stirring blend of beauty and truth that touches the heart to its core. The book and poem were written in love—to uplift and enlighten Black men.

In addition to referencing historical occurrences that define the Black man's experience in America—the book addresses the positive ways in which Black men should see themselves.

All books by Jean Dancy are available on Amazon, Barnes and Noble, and online everywhere books are sold.

To contact Jean Dancy...

InHousePublishingInfo@gmail.com

Instagram: @JeanDancy

www.ingramcontent.com/pod-product-compliance
Lightning Source LLC
Chambersburg PA
CBHW050250120526
44590CB00016B/2296